CLASSY SMOOTHIES

Carl Preston

Table of Contents

Classy Fruit and Oat Smoothie 1

Citrus Berry Good Smoothie 2

Breeze Smoothie 3

Creamy Breakfast Smoothie 4

Orange Flax Smoothie 5

Green Tea Smoothie 6

Live in Hawaii Smoothie 7

Avocado Smoothie 8

Mango-Coconut Smoothie 9

Mango Smoothie 10

Passion Smoothie 11

Greenfields Smoothie 12

Peanut Jelly Smoothie 13

Pineapple Glory Smoothie 14

Pomegranate Red Moon Smoothie 15

Pomegranate Berry Smoothie 16

Raspberry-Avocado Crazy Smoothie 17

Thermo-Nuclear Smoothie 18

Go Berry Nuts Smoothie 19

Strawberry Fields Smoothie 20

Tofu Tropicana Smoothie 21

Life in the Tropic Smoothie 22

Happy Wake-Up Smoothie 23

Banana Force Smoothie 24

Banana Spices Smoothie 25

Greenford Smoothie 26

Green Days Pineapple Smoothie 27

Ready to pack Smoothie 28

Creamonut Man Go Passionate smoothie 29

Peachy Melba smoothie 30

Silky Cranrasp smoothie 31

Manganana smoothie 32

BreakBerryFast smoothie 33

TropicFast smoothie 34

Clementine Festival Reception smoothie 35

Nottingham Forest smoothie 36

Zeus smoothie 37

Bone Strength smoothie 38

Good Heart smoothie 39

Averry smoothie 40

Mint Deluxe pineapple smoothie 41

Berry Oat Smoothie 42

Raspberry Coconut Smoothie 43

Full Detox Green Smoothie 44

Apple Pie Goodness Smoothie 45

Almond Butter Blueberry Smoothie 46

Chocolate Festival Smoothie 47

Cake Batter Crazy Smoothie 48

Vegan Brownie smoothie 49

Carrot Cake Madness Smoothie 50

Holiday Detox Apple Smoothie 51

Creamy Date Smoothie 52

Spiced Pumpkin Halloween Smoothie 53

Papaya Ginger Smoothie	54
Almonge Honey-Flavored Smoothie	55
Pure Blast Smoothie	56
Watermelon Blessing Smoothie	57
Banana Pear Smoothie	58
Spinaberry Smoothie	59
Citrus Energy-Boosting Smoothie	60
Beet and Strawberry Smoothie	61
Wild Blueberry Soy Punch	62
Strawberry Yogurt-Based Smoothie	63
Coffee chia smoothie	64
Detoxifying green smoothie recipe	65
Beetroot and blood orange smoothie	66
Spinach, avocado, lime and mint green smoothie	67
Citrus and ginger flu-Killer smoothie	68
Chialmond post-workout smoothie	69
New Roon-Go turmeric smoothie	70
Pear Berry Weight-Loss Smoothie	71
Green Tea Cinnamon Smoothie	72
Cherry Berry Merry Ginger Smoothie	73
Mangwi Smoothie	74
Papaya Ginger Mint	75
Blueberry Protein Smoothie	76
Sweet Spinach Smoothie	77
Metabolism-Boost Smoothie	78
Non-Alcoholic Mojito Smoothie	79
Vegan Vanilla Milkshake Smoothie	80
Chocolate Banana Berry Protein Smoothie	81

Cinnamon Apple Smoothie 82

Cinnamon Bun Smoothie 83

Chocolate Coconut Water Smoothie 84

Chocolate Banana Cashew Smoothie... 85

Chocolate Spinach Smoothie 86

Piña Colada Smoothie 87

Celery and Blueberry Smoothie 88

Avocado-Pear Smoothie... 89

Almond Strawberry Banana Yogurt Smoothie 90

Morning Workout Protein Smoothie 91

The Glowing Green Smoothie 92

Banana Berry Peanut Butter Broccoli Smoothie 93

Carrot-Ginger-Orange Smoothie 94

Fig Honey Yoghurt Smoothie 95

Chocolate Strawberry Banana Smoothie 96

Vegan Mint Chocolate Chip Shake 97

Velvety Butternut Cinnamon Date Smoothie 98

Vegan Glow Pink Power Detox Smoothie 99

Lime and Coconut Green Smoothie 100

Health Nut Blueberry Smoothie... 101

Mixed Berry Smoothie 102

No Banana Berry Green Smoothie 103

Oatmeal raisin cookie green smoothie 104

Classy Fruit and Oat Smoothie

Ingredients
- 1 cup of chopped strawberries
- 1 slice-cut banana
- 1/4 raw almonds small cup
- 1/2 small cup of oats
- 1 cup of low-fat vanilla yogurt
- 1 maple syrup teaspoon

Preparation
1. Drop into blender.

Citrus Berry Good Smoothie

Ingredients
- 1 1/4 cups of berries
- 3/4 cup low-fat yogurt (plain version)
- 1/2 cup orange juice
- 2 tablespoons of fat-free dry milk
- 1 tablespoon of toasted wheat germ
- 1 honey tablespoon
- 1/2 teaspoon of vanilla extract

Preparation
1. Put berries, yogurt, orange juice, dry milk, wheat germ, honey and vanilla in the blender and blend-mix until smooth.

Breeze Smoothie

Ingredients
- 1 small chopped cucumber
- 2 peeled kiwis
- 1 cup of ginger-flavored kombucha
- 1/2 cup of low-fat Greek yogurt
- 2 tablespoons fresh cilantro leaves
- 6 ice cubes

Preparation
1. Combine cucumber, kiwis, kombucha, yogurt, cilantro and ice cubes in blender; blend until it gets smooth. Serve the smoothie immediately.

Creamy Breakfast Smoothie

Ingredients
- 1 cup cold coconut water, no added sugar
- 1 cup nonfat vanilla Greek yogurt
- 1 cup frozen or fresh mango chunks
- 3 tablespoons frozen orange juice concentrate
- 2 cups ice

Preparation
1. Blend coconut water, yogurt, mango, orange juice concentrate and ice in a blender until smooth.

Orange Flax Smoothie

Ingredients
- 2 cups of frozen peach slices
- 1 cup of carrot juice
- 1 cupof orange juice
- 2 tablespoons full of ground flaxseed
- 1 tablespoon with plenty of chopped fresh ginger

Preparation
1. Combine peaches, carrot juice, orange juice, flaxseed and ginger in blender. Smooth out the mix. Serve immediately.

Green Tea Smoothie

Ingredients
- 3 cups of frozen grapes (white ideally)
- 2 packed cups of baby spinach
- 1 1/2 cups with cooled brewed green tea
- 1 medium ready to eat avocado
- 2 teaspoons full of honey

Preparation
1. Put together grapes, spinach, green tea, avocado and honey in the blender; blend it until smooth. Serve immediately.

Live in Hawaii Smoothie

Ingredients
- 1 cup of chopped pineapple
- 1/2 cup of peeled papaya (diced)
- 1/4 cup of guava nectar.
- 1 tablespoon with lime juice
- 1 teaspoon full of grenadine.
- 1/2 cup ice

Preparation
1. Place ingredients in the order listed in a blender. Pulse three times to chop the fruit, after this blend until smooth. Serve.

Avocado Smoothie

Ingredients
- 1 1/4 cups cold unsweetened almond milk (or coconut)
- 1 ready to eat avocado
- 1 ripe banana
- 1 sliced sweet apple
- 1 small stalk celery, chopped well.
- 2 cups with kale leaves or spinach
- 1 1-inch piece peeled fresh ginger
- 8 ice cubes

Preparation
1. Blend milk beverage, avocado, banana, apple, celery, kale (or spinach), ginger and ice in a blender until very smooth.

Mango-Coconut Smoothie

Ingredients
- 1/2 cup full of coconut water
- 1/3 cup with low-fat cottage cheese
- 1 cup of chopped kale
- 1 cup with frozen banana slices
- 1/2 cup of frozen mango
- 1 flaxseed tablespoon
- 1-2 teaspoons with maple syrup or honey

Preparation
1. Add coconut water and cottage cheese to the blender, then add kale, banana, mango, flaxseed. Blend until smooth.

Mango Smoothie

Ingredients
- 1 cup of chopped peeled mango
- 1/3 cup full of peach sorbet
- 1/2 cup nonfat vanilla yogurt
- 1/4 cup with orange juice
- 1/8 teaspoon orange-flower water

Preparation
1. Place ingredients in the order listed above in a blender. Pulse twice to chop mango, stir well, then blend the mix until smooth.

Passion Smoothie

Ingredients
- 1 ripe mango. Make sure it is peeled and diced
- 2/3 cup of low fat vanilla yogurt
- 1/3-1/2 cup frozen passion fruit juice
- 1/4 cup of water
- 2 ice cubes, well crushed

Preparation
1. Combine mango, yogurt, 1/3 cup juice concentrate, water and crushed ice in the blender machine; cover and blend the mix until it becomes smooth and frothy. Add more concentrate, if desired. Serve immediately.

Greenfields Smoothie

Ingredients
- 1 cup with properly chopped honey melon
- 1/3 cup of chopped kiwi
- 1/2 sliced ripe banana
- 1/4 cup with white grape juice
- 1/2 teaspoon full of ginger juice
- 2 teaspoons with lime juice
- 1/3 cup of lemon sorbet
- 1/2 cup of ice cubes (crushed)

Preparation
1. Place ingredients in the order listed above in a blender. Pulse three times to chop fruit, then blend until it becomes evenly smooth. Serve now.

Peanut Jelly Smoothie

Ingredients
- 1/2 cup low-fat milk
- 1/3 cup nonfat plain Greek yogurt
- 1 cup full of baby spinach
- 1 cup with frozen banana slices
- 1/2 cup with deliciously frozen strawberries
- 1 tablespoon containing natural peanut butter
- 1-2 teaspoons of maple syrup or honey

Preparation
1. Add milk and yogurt to a blender, add spinach, banana, strawberries, peanut butter and sweetener. Blend and smooth out.

Pineapple Glory Smoothie

Ingredients
- 1 cup cubed fresh canned pineapple
- 1/4 cup with frozen pineapple-orange-juice
- 1/2 cup fat free vanilla yogurt
- 1/4 cup of water
- 2 crushed ice cubes

Preparation
1. Combine pineapple, pineapple-orange-juice concentrate, yogurt, water and ice cubes in the blender; blend them until smoothed evenly and become frothy.

Pomegranate Red Moon Smoothie

Ingredients
- 2 cups frozen mixed berries
- 1 cup pomegranate juice
- 1 medium banana
- 1/2 cup nonfat cottage cheese
- 1/2 cup water

Preparation
1. Combine mixed berries, pomegranate juice, banana, cottage cheese and water in a blender; blend until smooth. Serve immediately.

Pomegranate Berry Smoothie

Ingredients
- 2 cups of frozen mixed berries
- 1 cup with pomegranate juice
- 1 medium banana
- 1/2 cup with nonfat cottage cheese
- 1/2 cup water

Preparation
1. Combine the mixed berries, pomegranate juice, banana, cottage cheese and water in a blender; blend until smooth.

Raspberry-Avocado Crazy Smoothie

Ingredients
- 1 avocado, peeled and pitted
- 3/4 cup orange juice
- 3/4 cup raspberry juice
- 1/2 cup frozen raspberries, (not thawed)

Preparation
1. Puree avocado, orange juice, raspberry juice and raspberries in a blender until smooth.

Thermo-Nuclear Smoothie

Ingredients
- 1 cup with frozen berries
- 1/2 banana
- 1/2 cup with concentrate apple juice
- 1/4 cup of tofu

Preparation
1. Mix berries, banana, apple juice concentrate and tofu in a blender machine; blend it until smooth and silky.

Go Berry Nuts Smoothie

Ingredients
- 10 frozen big strawberries
- 1 cup full of almond milk
- 1/2 cup full of tofu
- 2 sugar tablespoons

Preparation
1. Mixing strawberries, almond-made milk , tofu and sugar or sweetener into the machine. Blend until well frothy and smooth during 1 minute. Drop into a tall glass.

Strawberry Fields Smoothie

Ingredients
- 1 cup of nice frozen Strawberries, partially thawed
- 1 cup with buttermilk
- 1/2 cup full of frozen cranberry juice
- 2 crushed ice cubes
- 1 sugar teaspoon

Preparation
1. Mix strawberries, add buttermilk, drop cranberry juice and crushed ice into the blender; cover and blend until smooth and bubbly. Add sugar.

Tofu Tropicana Smoothie

Ingredients
- 2 cups of thin-diced frozen mango
- 1 1/2 cups pineapple juice concentrate
- 3/4 cup of tofu
- 1/4 cup lime juice
- 1 teaspoon of grated lime zest

Preparation
1. Put together mango, pineapple juice concentrate, tofu, lime juice and lime zest in the blender device; blend it until smooth. Serve now.

Life in the Tropic Smoothie

Ingredients
- 1 cup with cube-chopped pineapple. Ideally fresh. Canned is also acceptable.
- 1 sliced good size banana.
- 1/2 cup of tofu, (low-fat yogurt can be used as well)
- 1/3 cup frozen passion fruit concentrate
- 1/2 cup of fresh water
- 2 big ice cubes
- 1 wheat or oat bran tablespoon

Preparation
1. Mix pineapple, banana, tofu, passion fruit, water, ice cubes and bran in the blender; cover and blend until it gets well creamy.

Happy Wake-Up Smoothie

Ingredients
- 1 1/4 cups of orange juice
- 1 whole big banana
- 1 1/4 cups frozen raspberries, blackberries, blueberries and/or strawberries
- 1/2 cup low-fat tofu, or fat-free yogurt
- 1 sugar tablespoon

Preparation
1. Mix orange juice, banana, berries, tofu and add sugar in the machine; blend until creamy.

Banana Force Smoothie

Ingredients
- 1 1/4 orange juice cups from concentrate
- 1 medium sliced size banana
- 1 cup of frozen blueberries, blackberries or raspberries
- 1/2 cup of tofu
- 2 crushed ice cubes
- 1 sugar tablespoon

Preparation
1. Put together orange juice, banana, chosen berries, tofu and crushed ice in the blender machine. Sweeten with sugar.

Banana Spices Smoothie

Ingredients
- 2 ripe medioum sized bananas
- 2 cups full of vanilla kefir
- 1/2 teaspoon of cinnamon
- 1/8 teaspoon with nutmeg
- 1/8 teaspoon ground allspice
- 12 ice middle-sized cubes

Preparation
1. Mix kefir, bananas, cinnamon, ground nutmeg, allspice and ice cubes in a blender. Blend!

Greenford Smoothie

Ingredients
- 2 ripe medium bananas
- 1 ripe pear or apple, peeled if desired, chopped
- 2 cups chopped kale leaves, tough stems removed (see Notes)
- 1/2 cup cold orange juice
- 1/2 cup cold water
- 12 ice cubes
- 1 tablespoon ground flaxseed (see Notes)

Preparation
1. Place bananas, pear (or apple), kale, orange juice, water, ice cubes and flaxseed in a blender. Pulse a few times, then puree until smooth, scraping down the sides as necessary.

Green Days Pineapple Smoothie

Ingredients
- 1/2 cup unsweetened almond milk
- 1/3 cup nonfat plain Greek yogurt
- 1 cup baby spinach
- 1 cup frozen banana slices (about 1 medium banana)
- 1/2 cup frozen pineapple chunks
- 1 tablespoon chia seeds
- 1-2 teaspoons pure maple syrup or honey (optional)

Preparation
1. Add almond milk and yogurt to a blender, then add spinach, banana, pineapple, chia and sweetener (if using); blend until smooth.

Ready to pack Smoothie

Ingredients
- 1 cup frozen mixed happy berries
- 1/2 massive banana
- 1/2 cup apple juice
- 1/4 cup silken tofu

Preparation
1. Mix the berries, banana, apple juice and tofu in a blender machine. Do it!

Creamonut Man Go Passionate smoothie

Ingredients
- 200ml full of coconut milk
- 5 tbsp coco milk yogurt
- 1 big banana
- 1 tbsp of flaxseed, sunflower and pumpkin seed
- 125g of frozen mango pieces
- 1 passion fruit cup

Preparation
1. Pour everything into 1 tall glass. Crack on with the blender!.Go for it!!!

Peachy Melba smoothie

Ingredients
- 400g can of peach halves
- 110g frozen berries.
- 90ml of orange juice from concentrate
- 140ml of fresh custard

Preparation
1. Drain peaches and place in a blender with berries. Add orange juice concentrate and custard and whizz together.
2. Pour over ice, garnish with some more custard and a few berries. Serve quite cool.

Silky Cranrasp smoothie

Ingredients
- 175ml of juiced cranberries
- 170g of frozen raspberries
- 100ml of whole-fat milk
- 175ml of plain yogurt
- 1 tbsp of sugar
- mint leaves, as serving suggestion

Preparation
1. Put together all the ingredients into the blender and press power until it gets smooth. Pour into glasses and serve topped with mint leaves.

Manganana smoothie

Ingredients
- 1 large mango
- 1 large banana
- 550ml of orange juice from concentrate
- 3 ice cubes

Preparation
1. Cut the mango flesh into chunks. Chop banana. Place ingredients into a blender, then process until it gets thick and smooth.

BreakBerryFast smoothie

Ingredients
- 1 small banana
- 150g blackberries, blueberries or strawberries
- apple juice from concentrate
- Honey

Preparation
1. Slice the banana and add the berries. Whizz until it gets smooth. Pour in juice or water to make the consistency you prefer while the smoothie is being shaken.

TropicFast smoothie

Ingredients
- 4 passion fruits
- 1 chopped banana
- 1 medium size mango, chopped
- 275ml orange juice
- 5 ice cubes

Preparation
1. Scoop the pulp off the passion fruits into the blender and then add the banana, mango and orange juice from concentrate. Blend until smooth. Drink immediately, leaving the ice cubes floating on top.

Clementine Festival Reception smoothie

Ingredients
- 24 clementines
- 2 small, ripe mangoes
- 2 ready to eat small bananas
- 450g tub whole milk (you can also use fat-free yogurt)
- 4 handful of ice cubes

Preparation
1. Cut clementines in halves and squeeze out the juice Peel off mangoes, slice away the fruit from the stone, then chop flesh into big pieces. Slice the bananas.
2. Put clementine juice, mango flesh, bananas, yogurt and ice cubes into ablender and until smooth. Serve.

Nottingham Forest smoothie

Ingredients
- A few frozen fruits of the forest
- One medium size sliced banana
- fruits of the forest yogurt (fat free ideally)

Preparation
1. Drop everything in a food processor with fruits of the forest yogurt.

Zeus smoothie

Ingredients
- 1 roughly chopped orange
- 1 long carrot, roughly chopped
- 2 sticks of roughly chopped celery.
- 50g mangoes, roughly chopped
- 200ml water

Preparation
1. Put all the ingredients into the blender, top up with water, blend until smooth.

Bone Strength smoothie

Ingredients
- ½ chopped avocado
- Spinach leaves
- Kale leaves (washed)
- 600g of pineapple pieces
- 12cm roughly chopped cucumber
- 330ml of coconut water

Preparation
1. Put together avocado, spinach, kale, pineapple and cucumber into the blender. Top with coconut water, then blend until it gets smooth.

Good Heart smoothie

Ingredients
- 2 small beetroots: roughly chopped
- 1 small apple
- 55g blueberries
- 1 1/4 tbsp grated ginger
- 330ml water

Preparation
1. Put together the beetroot, apple, blueberries and ginger in a blender, top up with water then blend it smooth.

Averry smoothie

Ingredients
- ½ avocado cut into chunks
- 175g halved strawberries
- 5 tbsp low-fat natural yogurt
- 175ml semi-skimmed milk
- lemon or lime juice
- honey

Preparation
1. Put ingredients in a blender. When too thick, add some water.

Mint Deluxe pineapple smoothie

Ingredients
- 175g peeled, chopped pineapple
- mint leaves
- 60g baby spinach leaves
- 20g oats
- 2 1/2 tbsp linseeds
- handful cashew nuts
- fresh lime juice

Preparation

Put ingredients in the blender with 175ml water and leave it on until smooth. If it's too thick, add more water (but never more than 350 ml).

Berry Oat Smoothie

Ingredients
- ½ cup rolled oats
- 1 cup of semi-skimmed milk
- ½ cup full of frozen berries
- 2 tablespoons of honey
- ⅓ cup vanilla yogurt
- ¼ cup of ice

Preparation
1. Add all ingredients to a mixer. Cover and pulse until ice breaks up, then puree until it gets smooth. Add sweetener.

Raspberry Coconut Smoothie

Ingredients
- 1 cup of coconut milk
- 1 medium-sized banana, peeled and frozen
- 2 teaspoons of coconut extract
- 1 cup of frozen raspberries

Preparation
1. Add coconut milk, the frozen banana slices and coconut extract to the blender. Keep on for 1-2 minutes until smooth. Add frozen raspberries and continue smoothing out.
2. Pour into a serving glass, topped with a few of raspberries and shredded coconut.

Full Detox Green Smoothie

Ingredients
- 1 stalk of kale
- 1 cup of baby spinach
- ½ seedless lemon (keep skin on)
- ½ inch of peeled ginger
- 4 inch piece of peeled cucumber
- ¼ cup of very fresh parsley
- 1 peeled and chopped pear
- A few mint leaves
- 1 Daily Good Greens powder pack
- 3/4 cup water

Preparation
1. Mix all ingredients in a blender and keep on until smooth.

Apple Pie Goodness Smoothie

Ingredients:
- 2 red apples (core free)
- 1 big frozen banana
- 1 1/2 cup ice
- 1 cup ofalmond milk
- 1/2 cup of full-fat Greek yogurt
- 1 teaspoon of thinly ground cinnamon
- ¼ teaspoonof ground nutmeg
- 1/8 teaspoon of ground ginger
- 1/8 teaspoon of ground cloves

Preparation
1. Add ingredients to blender. Keep pressing ON until combined and smoothly shaken.

Almond Butter Blueberry Smoothie

Ingredients:
- 1 peeled banana
- 1 cup of frozen blueberries
- 1/2 cup with almond butter
- 1/2 cup with fat-free yogurt
- 3/4 cup full of almond milk
- 3 dates boneless and chopped
- 2 ice cups

Preparation:
1. Mix all ingredients in a blender machine; purée on high power until it gets smooth. Add the ice cubes and blend it until it gets consistent enough.

Chocolate Festival Smoothie

Ingredients
- 1 tablespoon of raw honey
- 1 medium sized banana
- 2 tablespoons of peanut butter
- 1½ tablespoons of cacao powder
- ½ cup of almond milk.

Preparation
1. Microwave honey for 5-10 seconds. Make a puree with honey, banana, peanut butter, cacao and almond milk in a blender until it gets smooth.

Cake Batter Crazy Smoothie

Ingredients
- 2 cups of ice
- 1 cup plain or vanilla yogurt
- ⅔ cup pf yellow cake mix, preferably dry
- ⅔ cup of milk
- chocolate syrup, sprinkles

Preparation
1. Add ice, yogurt, cake mix, and milk to a blender. Keep ON until smooth (crushing free).
2. If too thick add a few milk tablespoons and press ON until to desired consistency. Serve immediately. Add chocolate sprinkles and syrup.

Vegan Brownie smoothie

Ingredients
- 2 cups of almond, soy or your preferred milk.
- 1 frozen chopped banana
- 4 pitted dates
- 2 big tablespoons of raw cacao powder
- 2 massive tablespoons of coconut manna

Preparation
1. Blend.Serve.

Carrot Cake Madness Smoothie

Ingredients:
- 1 large banana, diced and frozen
- 1 cup of diced carrots
- 1 cup of almond milk
- 1/2 cup of plain Greek yogurt
- 2 medium teaspoons of maple syrup
- 1/4 teaspoon of cinnamon (ground)
- Small teaspoon of ground ginger
- Small teaspoon of nutmeg

Preparation:
1. Add everything a blender and press ON for 30-60 seconds until smooth. If too thick, add 1/4 cup of almond milk. Serve and garnish with optional toppings.

Holiday Detox Apple Smoothie

Ingredients
- 1 banana
- 1-2 cups kale
- 1 cup of apple cider
- 1 cup of ice
- 1/8 teaspoon of cinnamon
- Pomegranate seeds to top the smoothie with

Preparation
1. Blend all ingredients together. Use water replacing ice to achieve juice texture instead of smoothie texture. Drop in a dash of cinnamon, top it with pomegranate and serve.

Creamy Date Smoothie

Ingredients
- ¾ cup whole fat milk
- 1/2 cup pitted dates
- ½ cup cup ice

Preparation
1. Place the milk and dates in a blender. Cover until the dates have softened. Add ice and blend until frothy.

Spiced Pumpkin Halloween Smoothie

Ingredients
- 1 Ice cup
- 3/4 cup whole fat milk
- 1/3 cup full of pumpkin puree
- 1 honey tbsp
- 1/8 tbsp of ground nutmeg

Directions
1. Put ice, milk, pumpkin puree, nutmeg and honey into the machine blender. Blend until frothy.

Papaya Ginger Smoothie

Ingredients
- 1 ½ cups of chunked papaya (ideally chilled)
- 1 ¼ ice cup
- ½ cup fat free Greek yogurt
- 2 tbsp of freshly peeled ginger (well chopped)
- Half a lemon juice
- 1 tbsp of agave nectar
- Mint leaves

Preparation
1. Mix-blend papaya, ice, yogurt, ginger, lemon juice, the nectar, and mint in a mixer until it becomes a consistent enough smoothie.

Almonge Honey-Flavored Smoothie

Ingredients
- 250 mL of vanilla-flavoured almond drink
- 125 mL orange juice from concentrate
- 1 whole lemon juice
- 1 whole lime juice
- 5 ice cubes
- 20 mL of honey

Preparation
1. Blend all ingredients together.

Pure Blast Smoothie

Ingredients
- peeled large grapefruit (seed free)
- 125 mL crushed pineapple
- 125 mL frozen strawberries
- 125 mL of fat-free Greek yogurt

Preparation
1. Put together all ingredients and blend.

Watermelon Blessing Smoothie

Ingredients
- 500 mL chopped watermelon (no seeds)
- 250 mL of strawberry juice
- 250 mL fat-free yogurt
- 5 ice cubes

Preparations
1. Put all the ingredients into the blender and press ON.

Banana Pear Smoothie

Ingredients
- 2 ready to eat pears, (chop them coarsely and remove seeds)
- 5 mL of ginger root
- medium sized banana
- 250 mL skimmed milk
- 6 ice cubes
- Sprinkle of cinnamon

Preparation
1. Mix and blend the ingredients

Spinaberry Smoothie

Ingredients
- 125 mL of fat free vanilla yogurt
- 500 mL of water
- large banana
- 250 gr of strawberries
- 500 mL of fresh spinach
- Honey

Preparation
1. Combine yogurt, water, banana, 250 gr of strawberries, spinach and honey. Blend it and pour to serve.

Citrus Energy-Boosting Smoothie

Ingredients
- 1 orange with removed seeds. Peeled.
- 1 seedless, chopped lemon
- spinach leaves
- 2 grated carrots
- 400 mL of almond milk
- 1 peeled peach (no stone)

Preparation
1. Blend all ingredients together.

Beet and Strawberry Smoothie

Ingredients
- 4 cooked and peeled beets
- 500 mL of coconut water
- 500 mL frozen strawberries
- 1 juiced whole lime

Preparation
1. Blend all ingredients together.

Wild Blueberry Soy Punch

Ingredients

- 2 cups of frozen wild blueberries
- 3/4 cups of vanilla soy milk
- 5 tbsp honey
- 1/8 tbsp of ground nutmeg
- Garnish:
- Mint leaves

Preparation

1. Blend honey with soy milk, add frozen wild blueberries and puree until smooth. Season with a dash of nutmeg.

Strawberry Yogurt-Based Smoothie

Ingredients

- 1 L of ready to eat strawberries
- 250 mL of fat free yogurt
- 125 mL of squeezed orange juice
- 1 tbsp of sugar
- 4 small strawberries with leaves
- 4 slices of orance (with the skin)

Preparation

1. Rinse and drain the strawberries and place them in a food processor or blender. Add the yogurt, orange juice and sugar. Process on the highest speed

Coffee chia smoothie

Ingredients
- 175ml of almond milk
- 1 medium sized banana
- 1 1/4 shots of coffee
- 2 1/3 tbsp of chia seeds
- 1 tsp of vanilla extract or vanilla powder

Preparation
1. Place everything except the seeds in the blender and blend. Poor into a glass then stir in the chia seeds. Let this mix sit for 10 minutes. Keep stirring every minute.

Detoxifying green smoothie recipe

Ingrdients
- 50g of pineapple
- 1 kiwi (skinned)
- 330ml of coconut water
- 3/4 avocado
- 7 spinach leaves
- 3/4 tsp of coconut oil

Preparation
1. Place everything in a blender and smooth out.

Beetroot and blood orange smoothie

Ingredients
- 1 small beetroot
- 2 big blood oranges
- 1 medium ready to eat avocado
- 1 ¼ tbs raw honey
- 1tsp vanilla extract
- 250ml of mineral water

Preparation
1. Scrub the beetroot and slice into quarters. Peel the blood oranges removing any pips. Scoop out the avocado flesh. Add the beetroots, blood orange flesh, avocado flesh, raw honey, vanilla extract and water to the blender. Blend until smooth.

Spinach, avocado, lime and mint green smoothie

Ingredients
- 75g of watermelon flesh
- 50g baby spinach greens
- 250ml of coconut water
- 1 large apple (ideally sweet)
- 4 tbsp of avocado flesh
- 2 tbsp of fresh lime juice
- 8 large mint leaves
- 6 ice cubes

Preparation
1. Combine all of the ingredients in a mixer and blend until smooth and frothy.

Citrus and ginger flu-Killer smoothie

Ingredients
- 2 medium oranges (seedless and peeled)
- 3 tbsp. of lemon juice (fresh)
- 1 tsp of fresh ginger
- 3 tsp. of maple syrup
- 5 ice cubes
- Cayenne pepper

Preparation
1. Blend until smooth into the mixer.

Chialmond post-workout smoothie

Ingredients
- 250ml of almond milk
- 2 tbsp of rolled oats
- 2-3 Medjool dates
- 1 1/4 tbsp chia seeds
- 1 tbsp almond butter
- 1/2 tsp of cinnamon powder
- 1/4 tsp of vanilla extract
- 6 ice cubes

Preparation
1. In a mixer, combine all of the ingredients and blend until smooth and creamy.

New Roon-Go turmeric smoothie

Ingredients
- 1 large mango
- ½ frozen banana
- flesh from a coconut
- 250 ml of coconut water
- ½ tsp of grated turmeric
- 3 ice cubes

Preparation
1. Cut mango into chunks. Place in a blender with other ingredients and press ON until it gets creamy /

Pear Berry Weight-Loss Smoothie

Ingredients
- pear
- 1 peeled kiwi
- 1/4 ready to eat avocado
- 1 1/4 cup of frozen raspberries
- 1 ¼ cup of raw spinach
- 2 ounces of fat free vanilla Greek yoghurt
- 3/4 tbsp of flax meal
- 1 3/4 cups cold water

Preparation
1. Mix everything in a blender until smooth.

Green Tea Cinnamon Smoothie

Ingredients
- 1/2 cup of chilled green tea
- 1/2 cup of almond milk
- cinnamon tbsp.
- 1 tablespoon of honey
- 3/4 banana

Preparations
1. Add one to two scoops of ice to blender with all ingredients pressing ON until smooth.

Cherry Berry Merry Ginger Smoothie

Ingredients
- 1/4 cup of cherries (frozen)
- 1 cup of strawberries
- 3/4 cup of kale
- 1/6 cup walnuts
- 1 tbsp. full of wheat germ
- 1/2 tbsp. of grated ginger
- 1/2 cup of green tea

Preparations
1. Mix everything into a blender. Serve rapidly.

Mangwi Smoothie

Ingredients
- 3 ounces of fat-free vanilla yoghurt
- 1 1/4 cups of baby spinach
- 1/2 cup of frozen blueberries
- 1/2 cup of ripe mango (frozen)
- 1 peeled kiwi
- 1/4 cup full of kidney beans
- 1/6 cup of walnuts
- 1 teaspoon of flax meal
- 3/4 cup filled with cold water

Preparations
1. Pour all ingredients into the blender and mix.

Papaya Ginger Mint

Ingredients
- 1 peeled and chunked papaya
- 3/4 cup of ice cubes
- 1/2 cup of fat-free Greek yoghurt
- 1/2 tablespoon of fresh ginger
- 1/2 tbsp. of honey
- Juice from half a lemon
- Water to taste
- 5 fresh mint leaves plus 2 sprigs (garnishing)

Preparations
1. Blend papaya, ice, yoghurt, ginger, honey, and lemon juice into a blender. Add water, one tablespoon every time, until smooth and thinned as required by your taste. Mix in mint leaves. Garnish using mint leaves and sprigs.

Blueberry Protein Smoothie

Ingredients
- cup of vanilla almond milk
- 2 scoops of vanilla protein powder
- 1/2 cup with blueberries (frozen)
- 1 cup with plenty of spinach
- 1/2 cup fat-free Greek yogurt
- 4 Ice cubes

Preparations
1. Place all ingredients in a blender. Press ON for 30 seconds. Serve fast.

Sweet Spinach Smoothie

Ingredients
- cups full of spinach leaves
- 1 ready to eat pear (peeled)
- 15 grapes
- 175 grams of low fat Greek yoghurt
- 2 tbsp. of avocado (chopped)
- 2 tbsp of lime juice

Preparations
1. Combine all the ingredients until blended to the desired consistency.

Metabolism-Boost Smoothie

Ingredients
- 175 grams of fat free Greek yoghurt
- almonds
- 1/4 cup broccoli florets (stem free)
- 1 cup of frozen strawberries
- 1/3 cup of cannellini beans
- 3/4 cup filled with cooled green tea
- 1 tbsp. flax meal
- 1/4 cinnamon tbsp.

Preparations
1. Pour all ingredients into a mixer and smoothly blend. Add cinnamon on top.

Non-Alcoholic Mojito Smoothie

Ingredients
- 1/2 cup of soy milk
- medium sized frozen banana
- 1 cup baby spinach
- 1 teaspoon vanilla extract
- 1/2 small lime, juiced
- 1/2 cup fresh spearmint
- Ice cubes

Preparations
1. Combine soy milk, banana, spinach, vanilla, and lime juice in a high-speed blender.
2. Add spearmint and four or five ice cubes. Blend until smooth and creamy.
3. Taste, and add more spearmint or lime juice as desired.

Vegan Vanilla Milkshake Smoothie

Ingredients
- 1/2 cup soft tofu
- 1 cup vanilla soy milk
- 1 banana
- 1/2 tablespoon peanut butter

Preparations
1. Place everything in a blender and mix until smooth, about one minute. Enjoy!

Chocolate Banana Berry Protein Smoothie

Ingredients
- 85 grams plain non-fat Greek yoghurt
- 1 banana
- 1/2 cup blueberries
- 1/2 cup strawberries
- 1/2 cup raspberries
- 1/2 cup chocolate milk
- 1/2 cup water

Preparations
1. Place all ingredients in a blender and mix until smooth.
2. Enjoy immediately.

Cinnamon Apple Smoothie

Ingredients
- 8 ounces coconut water
- 4 raw almonds
- teaspoon vanilla extract
- 1 teaspoon ground cinnamon
- 1 cup chopped apple (about 1 medium apple)
- 1/2 scoop unsweetened protein powder
- 1 tablespoon flaxseed meal (ground flaxseed)

Preparations
1. Combine all ingredients into a blender, and pulse for approximately 10-15 seconds.
2. If you're going to drink it immediately, add three ice cubes to chill it. If you're preparing ahead of time, chill in the fridge overnight.

Cinnamon Bun Smoothie

Ingredients
- 1 frozen banana, cut into four pieces
- 1 cup unsweetened almond milk
- 1/2 teaspoon ground cinnamon
- 1/4 teaspoon vanilla extract
- 1/2 teaspoon pure maple syrup
- Cinnamon stick, for garnish

Preparations
1. Combine all ingredients in a blender. Blend until smooth, and add more almond milk if necessary.
2. Pour into a tall glass, add the cinnamon stick for garnish, and enjoy.

Chocolate Coconut Water Smoothie

Ingredients
- 8 ounces ZICO chocolate coconut water
- 1 banana, frozen
- 3 tablespoons raw hemp seeds

Preparations
1. Combine all ingredients in a blender, and mix well.
2. Top off with sliced banana and a sprinkle of raw hemp seeds if you wish.

Chocolate Banana Cashew Smoothie

Ingredients

- 85 grams. non-fat vanilla Greek yoghurt
- 1/2 frozen banana
- 1/4 avocado
- 1/2 cup spinach
- 1/2 cup chocolate soy milk
- 1/8 cup raw cashews
- 1/2 cup water
- For garnish:
- 3 dark chocolate chips

Preparations

1. Add ingredients to a blender (save three cashews for topping) and mix until smooth.
2. Pour into a glass.

Chocolate Spinach Smoothie

Ingredients
- 1 frozen banana, chopped into pieces
- 1 cup spinach
- 1/2 cup non-fat yogurt
- 1 cup chocolate almond milk
- Pinch of cinnamon, optional

Preparations
1. Blend all ingredients together until smooth and creamy.
2. Top off with cinnamon if you wish, and drink up!

Piña Colada Smoothie

Ingredients
- 3/4 cup fresh pineapple, diced
- 1/4 cup light coconut milk
- 1/2 small banana
- 1/4 cup crushed ice
- 1/4 teaspoon minced lemongrass
- 44msl rum, optional (adding rum adds 97 calories to the recipe)
- For garnish:
- 1 teaspoon unsweetened coconut flakes

Preparations
1. Combine all ingredients except the coconut flakes in a blender container and puree until smooth.
2. Top off with coconut flakes, and enjoy!

Celery and Blueberry Smoothie

Ingredients
- 2 cups fresh blueberries
- 1 banana
- 1 stalk of celery
- 1 cup water
- 1 cup orange juice
- Few cubes ice

Preparations
1. Pour the orange juice and water into the blender with the banana and blend. Add the blueberries and celery and blend again. Finally, add the ice cubes for a smooth consistency.

Avocado-Pear Smoothie

Ingredients
- 1 ripe, firm Hass avocado
- 1/2 cup (about 4 ounces) drained silken tofu
- 1 cup unsweetened pear juice
- 2 tablespoons honey
- 1/2 teaspoon pure vanilla extract
- 2 cups ice cubes

Preparations
1. Cut avocado in half lengthwise; remove pit, then score flesh into cubes. With a large spoon, scrape flesh into a blender.
2. Add tofu, pear juice, honey, and vanilla, and puree until smooth. Add ice; blend until smooth.
3. Divide among four glasses, and serve.

Almond Strawberry Banana Yogurt Smoothie

Ingredients
- 4 large strawberries
- 1/2 banana
- 1/2 cup blueberries
- 3 ounces soy yogurt
- 1 cup unsweetened soy milk
- 12 raw almonds
- 3 ice cubes

Preparations
1. Place all the ingredients in a blender or food processor and blend until smooth and creamy. Enjoy immediately.

Morning Workout Protein Smoothie

Ingredients
- 1/2 cup unsweetened vanilla almond milk
- 1/2 cup water
- 1/2 banana
- Dash of cinnamon
- 1 scoop of vanilla protein powder
- 1 to 2 drops of liquid Stevia, optional

Directions
1. Combine all ingredients in a blender and blend until smooth. Makes one serving.

The Glowing Green Smoothie

Ingredients

- 1 1/2 cups water
- 1 head organic romaine lettuce, chopped
- 3-4 stalks organic celery
- 1/2 head of a large bunch or 3/4 of a small bunch of spinach
- 1 organic apple, cored and chopped
- 1 organic pear, cored and chopped
- 1 organic banana
- Juice of 1/2 fresh organic lemon
- Optional: 1/3 bunch organic cilantro (stems OK) and 1/3 bunch organic parsley (stems OK)

Preparations

1. Add water and chopped head of romaine to blender. Blend at a low speed until smooth.
2. Add celery, apple, and pear and blend at high speed.
3. Add cilantro and parsley (which help chelate heavy metals out of your body).
4. Finish with banana and lemon.

Banana Berry Peanut Butter Broccoli Smoothie

Ingredients
- 1 frozen banana
- 6 frozen strawberries
- 4 raw broccoli florets
- 6 ounces vanilla Greek yogurt (or soy yogurt)
- 1/2 tablespoon smooth peanut butter
- 1/4 cup cold water

Preparations
1. Add ingredients to a blender and blend until smooth. Enjoy immediately!

Carrot-Ginger-Orange Smoothie

Ingredients
- 1 cup fresh, pure carrot juice (organic if possible)
- 1 organic orange, peeled
- 1 big handful of organic spinach
- 1 small square of ginger
- 1 to 2 handfuls of ice

Preparations
1. Place carrot juice, orange, spinach, and ginger in blender.
2. Blend on medium speed for about 30 seconds.
3. Add ice and finish blending.

Fig Honey Yoghurt Smoothie

Ingredients
- 1/2 cup unsweetened almond milk or unsweetened vanilla almond milk
- 1/2 cup non-fat Greek yoghurt
- 1 to 2 scoops of ice
- 4 fresh figs, stems removed and cut in half
- 1/2 banana
- 1 date, pitted
- 1 tablespoon honey
- 1 teaspoon fresh lemon juice
- Dash of cinnamon

Preparations
1. Add almond milk, yoghurt, ice, figs, and banana to a blender, and blend for about 20 to 30 seconds.
2. Add date, honey, lemon juice, and cinnamon, and blend again until fully combined. Serve immediately.

Chocolate Strawberry Banana Smoothie

Ingredients
- 5 frozen strawberries
- 1 frozen banana
- 1 cup spinach
- 6 ounces plain Greek yogurt (or soy yogurt)
- 1/2 cup chocolate soy milk
- 1/2 tablespoon peanut butter

Preparations
1. Blend all ingredients together until smooth and creamy. Enjoy!

Vegan Mint Chocolate Chip Shake

Ingredients
- 1 tablespoon raw cacao nibs
- 1/2 teaspoon vanilla extract
- 1/2 cup dairy-free vanilla ice cream
- 1 handful mint leaves (stems OK)
- 2 teaspoons or half a packet of Green Vibrance green food supplement (optional)
- 3 large ice cubes
- 1/2 cup or more unsweetened almond milk
- Pinch of Himalayan sea salt

Preparations
1. Cafe Gratitude, one of my favorite vegan restaurants in San Francisco, makes an incredible vegan mint chocolate chip shake dubbed "I am cool." The cafe might be closing, but I've been working for months to try to re-create the delicious shake that is vegan, sugar-free, and a healthy alternative to dairy shakes. If you don't have Green Vibrance or some other green food smoothie powder, feel free to leave it out of the recipe.
2. Combine all ingredients in a blender, and blend until smooth. Thin out with more almond milk if needed.

Velvety Butternut Cinnamon Date Smoothie

Ingredients:

- 1 cup + 1/2 cup almond milk
- 1 cup + 1/4 cup (packed) roasted butternut squash or 3/4-1 cup canned puréed squash
- 3-4 large Medjool dates, pitted
- 1 tablespoon chia seeds
- 1-2 teaspoons cinnamon, to taste
- 1.5 teaspoons pure vanilla extract
- 1/2 teaspoon ground ginger
- sprinkle of ground cloves
- 5-6 large ice cubes, or as needed

Preparations:

1. To cook the squash: Preheat oven to 400F and line a baking sheet with parchment paper. Slice the stem off the squash (optional) and slice the squash in half lengthwise. Scoop out the seeds with a spoon. Brush a bit of oil on the squash and sprinkle with a pinch of salt. Place squash on the baking sheet, cut side up, and roast for 35-50 minutes, until fork tender and golden brown on the bottom. Allow to cool.
2. For the smoothie: Add all smoothie ingredients into a high speed blender and blend on high until smooth, adjusting the spices as needed. Serve immediately & enjoy!

Vegan Glow Pink Power Detox Smoothie

Ingredients:
- 1 cup water or coconut water
- 1/2 medium avocado, pitted
- 2 celery stalks, roughly chopped
- 1 cup strawberries (frozen preferred), hulled if necessary
- 1 small/medium beet, ends trimmed and roughly chopped*
- 1 lemon, juiced (about 3 tablespoons or so)
- 1 tablespoon coconut oil
- 4 large ice cubes
- 1 apple (if sweeter smoothie is desired - optional), cored and roughly chopped

Preparations:
1. Steam beet if necessary before starting. See my tips in the headnote.
2. Add all ingredients into a high-speed blender and blend on high until smooth. Adjust sweetness if desired, adding an apple or liquid sweetener to taste if needed.

Lime and Coconut Green Smoothie

Ingredients
- Juice of 1 lime
- 1/2 cup coconut milk
- 1/2 cup coconut water
- 1/2 frozen banana
- 2 cups of spinach
- Ice (if you like your smoothie a little thicker)

Preparations
1. Juice your lime and measure out all of your other ingredients.
2. Layer them together in your blender and blend until smooth.
3. Garnish your glass with a little extra lime if you so desire.
4. Bottoms up.

Health Nut Blueberry Smoothie

Ingredients
- 1 frozen banana
- 1 cup frozen (or fresh) blueberries
- handful of fresh baby spinach
- 1 Tablespoon natural almond butter
- 1 Tablespoon unsweetened dried coconut
- 1 cup almond milk
- 3-5 cubes of ice

Preparations
1. Place all ingredients into a high powered blender and blend until smooth. If the smoothie is too thick, add a little more almond milk to get the consistency you like. Pour into a glass and enjoy.

Mixed Berry Smoothie

Ingredients:
- 150g frozen berries
- 1 banana
- 1 tsp honey
- 4 tbsp natural yoghurt
- 150ml orange juice

Preparation
1. Chop up the banana into manageable chunks, throw everything into a blender and blitz until smooth. If it seems a little thick add more juice, or if it's not quite creamy enough add more yoghurt. If you wish remove the berry seeds pass the smoothie through a sieve, but don't worry too much!

No Banana Berry Green Smoothie

Ingredients
- 1 cup packed baby spinach
- ½ cup frozen strawberry
- ½ cup frozen raspberries
- ½ cup non fat vanilla greek yogurt
- ½ cup orange juice

Preparations
1. Combine spinach, frozen strawberries, frozen raspberries, non fat vanilla greek yogurt, and a little orange juice into your blender or Vitamix.
2. Blend until smooth.
3. Drink immediately!

Oatmeal raisin cookie green smoothie

Ingredients
- 1 frozen banana
- 2 handfuls spinach
- 1/3 cup non-dairy milk (I used homemade almond milk)
- 1 medjool date, soaked and pitted (or 1 tbsp soaked raisins works too!)
- 2 tbsp oats + 2 tbsp oats, divided
- 1 tbsp almond butter
- 1/2 tsp cinnamon
- splash vanilla
- 1/8 tsp xanthan gun (optional but really helps give it a thick texture)
- 1 tbsp raisins, chopped

Preparation
1. Throw the banana, spinach, milk, date, 2 tbsp oats, almond butter, cinnamon and xanthan gum in a blender and blend until smooth.
2. Pour into a bowl and add in the other 2 tbsp oats and the chopped raisins and stir to distribute them throughout.

Printed in Great Britain
by Amazon